how did Nonnie get to Heaven?

by Arlene Michlin Bronstein

illustrated by Diana Torres

ASHLEY SPIRIT
publications

author Arlene Michlin Bronstein
illustrator Diana Torres

—— *Inspired by* ——

Liza Bates Macleod

&

**The poem "Gone from My Sight"
by Henry Van Dyke**

ASHLEY SPIRIT
publications

www.howdidnonniegettoheaven.com

to

Keith Bronstein

My Heaven on Earth

special thanks to

Arielle Eckstut
Steven Stark Lowenstein
Masayo Anton-Ozawa
Ellen Sandor
German Torres
Adrienne Weiss

Even though the Brown triplets looked exactly alike,
there was not much about them that was identical.

Dylan liked the color pink, big red hearts
and swimming underwater holding her nose.

Cameron liked the color yellow,
smiley faces and playing basketball.

And Zoey liked the color green,
peace signs and drawing rainbows.

The only thing they agreed on was
that their grandmother's chocolate
chip cookies were the best ever!

One beautiful, summer day, their mommy told them to get dressed because they were going to the park. She had packed a picnic lunch and was bringing their bathing suits just in case they had time to go to the lake.

They all piled in the van, buckled their seat belts and watched the familiar scenery of their little town.

"I remember going to "story hour"
at the library with Nonnie," said Dylan.
"I miss hearing her read us books."

Zoey pointed, "There's the knit shop where Nonnie made us sweaters." And Cameron added, "When I wear the sweater, I can almost feel her hugging me."

Nonnie was their grandmother
who had died three months ago.

When they saw the park, they couldn't wait to get out of the van. Zoey ran for the monkey bars and Cameron headed up the curly slide. Dylan jumped on a swing and mommy was pushing her.

Before long Zoey and Cameron wanted to get pushed too. Mommy worked hard to keep them all up in the air.

All of a sudden, Cameron said,
"I am so high, I think I can
touch heaven and see Nonnie!"

"Me too" said Dylan. "And so can I," cried Zoey. "We miss Nonnie!"

"I am sure Nonnie misses you too,"
sadly replied their mother.

"How did Nonnie get to heaven?" asked Cameron.

"I am not sure," Mommy said. "What do you think?"

Cameron replied, "I think she got on a swing,
just like this one and she pushed higher and higher
and then she jumped off into heaven!"

"I think she went on a giant trampoline," said Dylan. "I can see her bouncing harder and harder until finally she was able to reach out and touch the fluffy clouds."

"Wait. I know!" cried Zoey. "She got on top of a big rocketship, and she counted 3-2-1 and she launched into heaven!"

"Wow," said their mother.
"You have wonderful ideas. Let's talk more over lunch!"

She spread a large red and white blanket on
the ground and the girls opened the basket and
pulled out their peanut butter and jelly sandwiches.

Dylan liked hers whole. Zoey liked hers cut in half and
Cameron liked hers without any crust. They sat and ate
and thought about Nonnie and her trip to heaven.

"You know," said Dylan, "maybe when they planted Nonnie in the ground, there were some bean seeds under her and a giant beanstalk took her up to heaven."

"Or maybe," suggested Zoey, "she climbed up a very, very tall ladder, like the one grandpa uses to get up on the roof, and rung by rung, she climbed up to heaven!"

"I know!" said Cameron jumping up.
"She got hundreds and hundreds
of different colored balloons, and
she held onto them very tightly and
they gently lifted her up to heaven!"

"And," continued Dylan, "the air was filled with her perfumey smell and she would not be hungry because her purse was always filled with candy and she would not be lonely because her mom and dad and friends would be there to greet her..."

"And," Zoey said,
"Nonnie would give each of them a balloon!"

Mommy wiped away a tear as she listened
to her girls and their special thoughts.

"What do you think Mommy?" asked Zoey.

"Let's go to the beach and we can talk about it there!"

When they got to the beach, Dylan grabbed
her pail and began digging a deep hole.
Cameron started to build a sand castle and
Zoey jumped in and out of the waves.

After a few minutes, mommy called them over to look at a boat that was getting ready to leave the harbor. There were two people getting on the boat and one of them held the wheel and the other raised the sail.

It wasn't long before the boat headed out in the water.

As it moved away from the shore, it got smaller and smaller.
Mommy told the girls to keep watching the boat.

"It disappeared!" said Cameron.
"I can't see it anymore!" said Zoey
"Where did it go?" asked Dylan.

"I am not sure where it went," said Mommy, "but just because
we can't see it anymore, doesn't mean that the boat is gone."

At dinner the girls told Daddy about
their day and all the different ways they
thought that Nonnie got to heaven.

They kept talking all the way through getting on their PJs and brushing their teeth and washing their faces. As dad was tucking each of them into bed, Cameron asked, "So Daddy, how do you think Nonnie got to heaven?" Daddy kissed each of them on the head and he turned out the light.

"Well, I don't know how Nonnie got to heaven,
but I know one thing for sure." "What's that?" asked Zoey.

"I know that Nonnie is definitely in heaven, and she floated
there on all the loving memories you have of her!"

"She will always be up there watching over all of you."

"When someone is loved," Daddy said softly, "no matter
where they are, they can always be with you in your heart."

Dylan hugged her stuffed brown dog and Zoey hugged her little, elephant and Cameron stroked the ears of her favorite blue dog.

It had been a very special day and there was no doubt that
Nonnie would be there to give them hugs in their dreams.

the
END